# With These Hands

7 EARLY ADVANCED SOLOS FOR PIANO

DENNIS ALEXANDER

## Foreword

This collection of pieces was written close to a year following the very unexpected and untimely death of my handsome and talented son, Darren Andrew Alexander. Losing a child is a life-changing experience, and having dealt with the harsh reality of such a tragedy, I consequently have learned to appreciate even more what is truly important in day-to-day living. Fortunately, music has been and will always be a dominant influence in my daily existence. Following Darren's death, a good friend wrote the following words to me, which I still appreciate and treasure so much:

> "...through all of your hard work and effort you have given young people the gift of music. Music will be, for many of your students, one of the ways they develop their own spirit and soul. It will also be a way your students will be helped and healed during the hurts and losses they will inevitably face in their own lives."

What a journey this has been! The following collection is a musical tribute to the life of a very special young man who, during his short time on earth, managed to touch so many people with his sensitive and caring soul, his artistic talent and his love of nature and all things beautiful. Each piece in this collection represents something significant and meaningful in his life. I would like to thank Darren's mother, Christine, for her encouragement and help along the way when I needed an extra boost. Also, special thanks to my friends at Alfred Publishing Company for their assistance and compassion in bringing this project to completion. Upon finishing the last piece in this collection, entitled "Forever in Our Hearts," I went back to the beginning and counted the measures, realizing that it was shorter than the other pieces. Ironically, there were just 23 bars; Darren was 23 years old when he died. Somehow I knew that my guardian angel was there helping me out all along the way! Darren, this book is for you — please know that your presence here on earth is sorely missed, and that you are and always will be "Forever in Our Hearts." With much love, Mom and Dad.

## Contents

Darren loved animals. In his memory, Alfred Publishing Company will donate a portion of its profits from the sale of this collection to the Humane Society Animal Shelter in Missoula, Montana.

A recording of this collection with other pieces by Dennis Alexander is available on compact disc (*With These Hands* #18543).

With grateful appreciation to Lucien Hut for the cover photo – a hand sculpture done in 1997 by Darren Alexander of his own hands.

You are cordially invited to view a special webpage in memory of Darren at: www.blarg.net/~george1/darren.htm

# Sunset Soliloquy

## PROLOGUE

Dennis Alexander

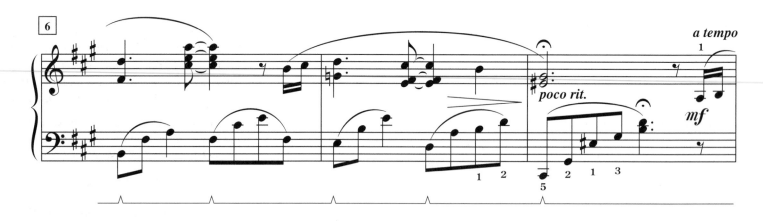

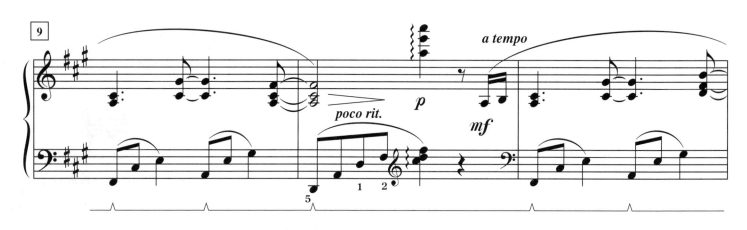

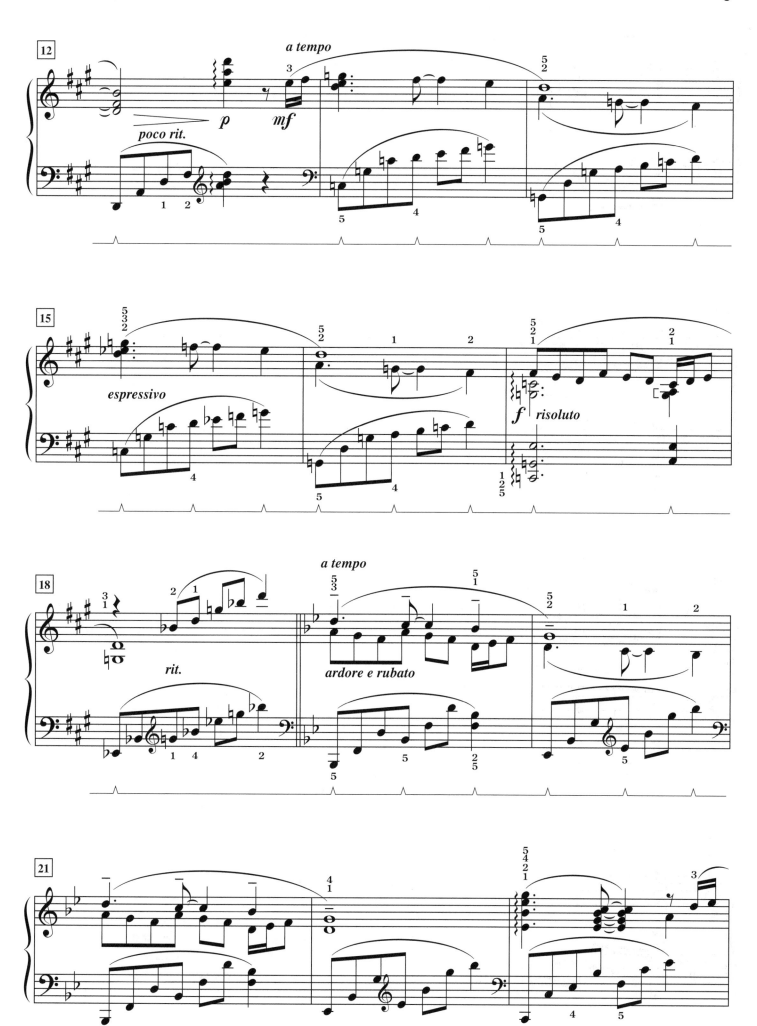

# Dolphin Quest

DENNIS ALEXANDER

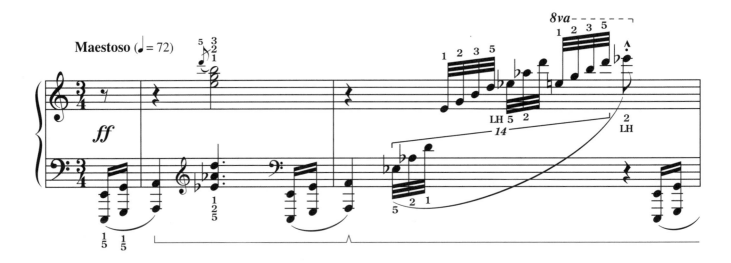

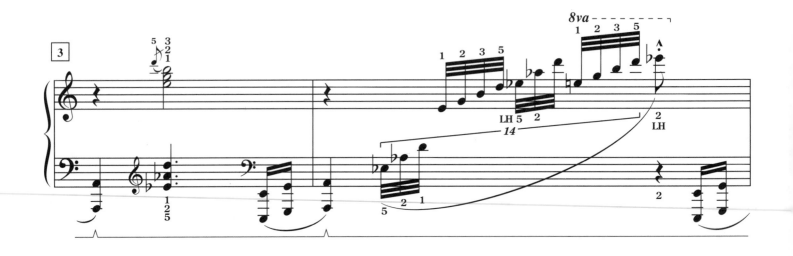

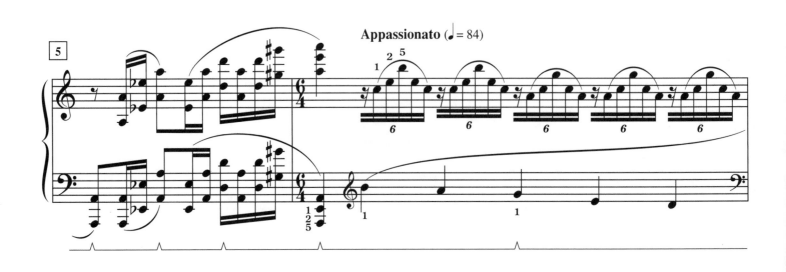

# Transcending All Time

Dennis Alexander

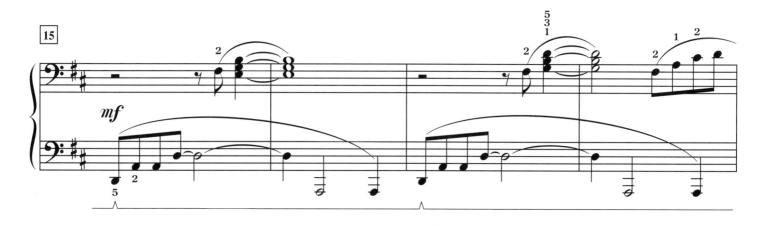

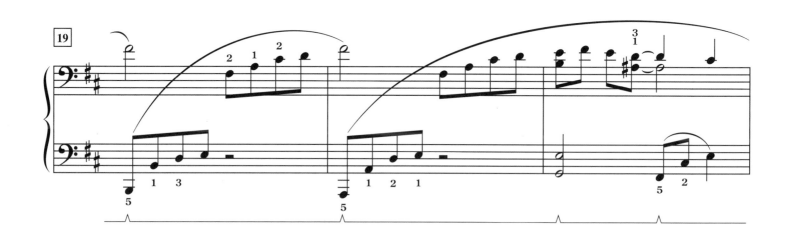

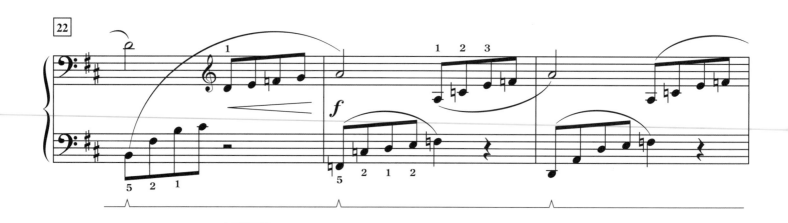

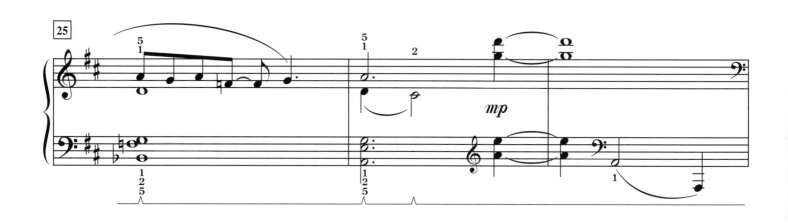

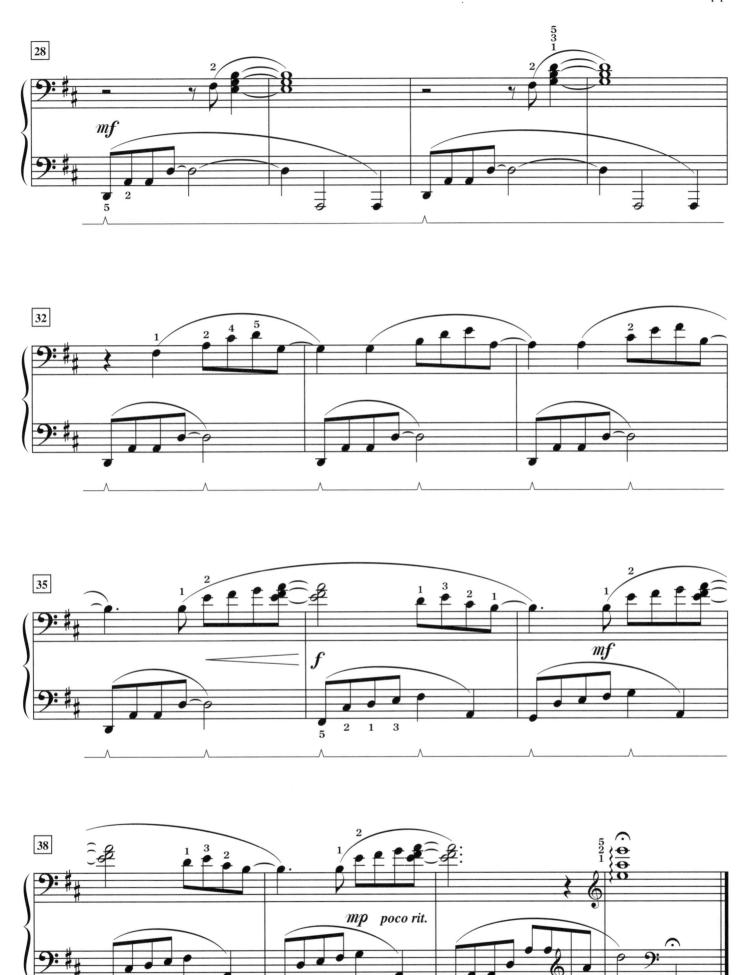

DEDICATED TO DARREN'S CANINE FRIENDS SASHA, WOLFGANG AND SERGEI

# Best Buddies

DENNIS ALEXANDER

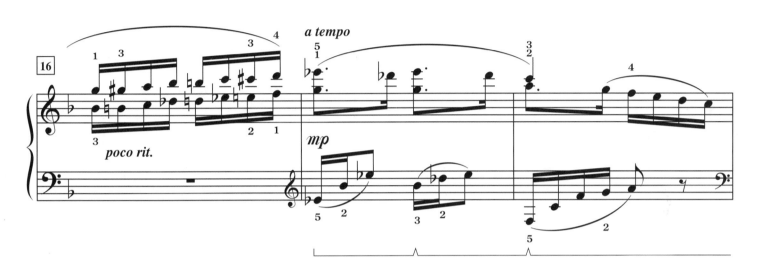

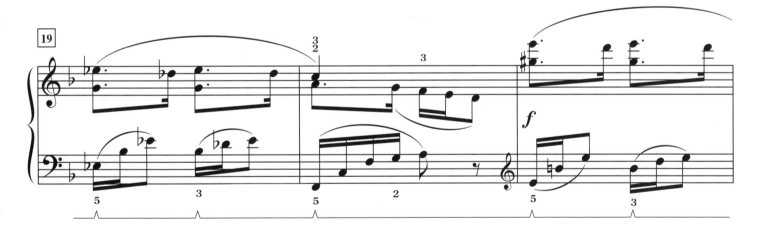

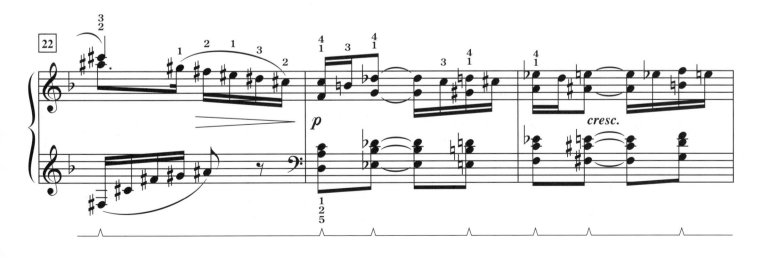

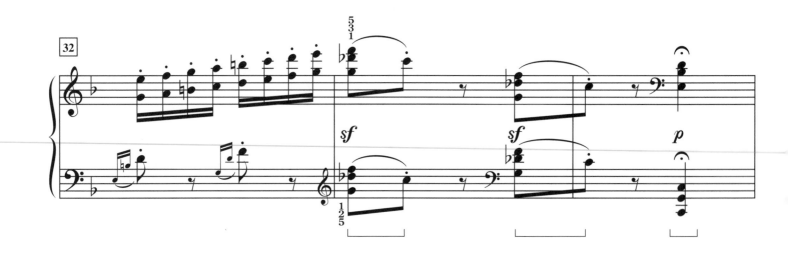

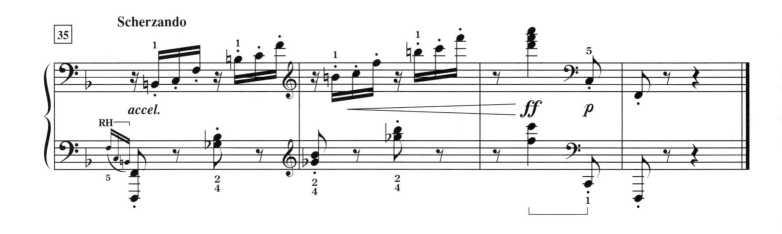

DEDICATED TO NANCY LONG

# Butterflies Are Free

"A butterfly lights beside us, like a sunbeam.
And for a brief moment its glory and beauty
belong to our world.

But then it flies on again, and though
we wish it could have stayed,
we feel so lucky to have seen it."

Author unknown

DENNIS ALEXANDER

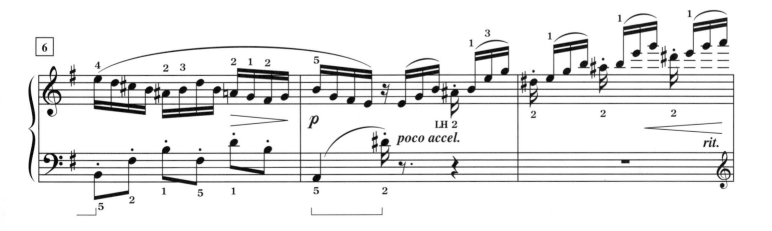

# Topaz Nocturne

Dennis Alexander

# Forever in Our Hearts

Epilogue

Dennis Alexander

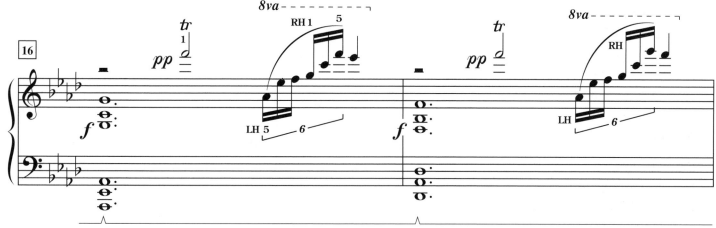

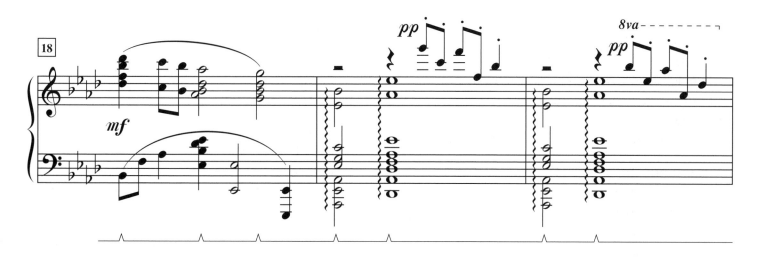

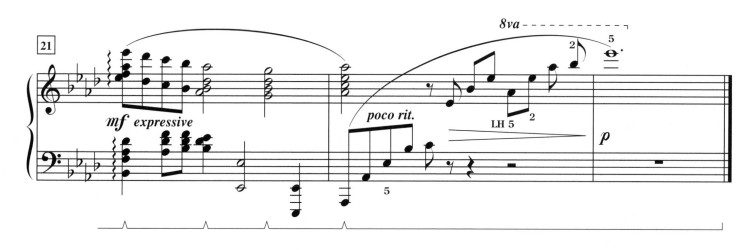

# Performance Notes

## Sunset Soliloquy

This prologue is a serene, contemplative piece, inspired by a photograph taken of Darren high atop a mountain overlooking the Missoula, Montana valley. Darren always loved this picture; the calm skies and peaceful surroundings evoke memories of his kind and gentle spirit as well as his great love of nature and beautiful sunsets! In fact, some of his most inspired photographs were taken of sunsets in the mountains of Montana as well as those along the beaches of Florida. Performance requirements include much freedom of expression, beautiful legato touch and sensitivity to the intricate voicing needed in the right hand in measures 27–30. Take time to expand the *ff* in measure 31. Careful listening and attention to pedaling in measures 35–39 will help create the necessary color of this beautiful sunset.

## Dolphin Quest

One of Darren's dreams was to someday ride on the back of a dolphin! Perhaps he is even living this exciting adventure in his new "world." He loved water and marine life in general; in fact, when he was quite young he thought seriously about becoming a marine biologist. "Dolphin Quest" is a powerful virtuosic showpiece. Block out the patterns of each hand in the opening arpeggios and carefully observe pedal markings. The opening bars suggest a dolphin leaping out of the depths of the ocean. In the middle section, listen carefully and project the melody line shared by both hands as the dolphin surges through the ocean waves.

## Transcending All Time

This is a very "personal" solo in that the first three notes of the LH outline "D-A-A," for Darren Andrew Alexander. He was a great fan of Broadway musicals and spent many hours listening to music of all styles. Among his favorite Broadway hits was the song "Beauty and the Beast." I have extracted the first five notes of this song as a motive for the RH melody (measure 5) and combined it with the opening LH pattern. The solo closes with this same rising LH three-note motive appearing twice in measure 40, followed by three last notes, just before the final octave, that outline "D-A-D."

## Best Buddies

Animals were always very special to Darren, and his canine friends included Sasha, Sergei (golden retrievers) and Wolfgang (cocker spaniel). Their exuberant and playful personalities were always at a peak the minute they saw him! Darren loved nothing more than to have his "buddies" sleep on his bed and, of course, the dogs were spoiled by his generous attention! The parallel 6ths in the RH (measures 5–8) need to be *leggiero*, delicate and free from any tension in the wrist. Work to create a playful character, with particular attention to pedaling.

## Butterflies are Free

Darren was blessed to have discovered a wonderful friend at the Ringling School of Art and Design. Nancy Long came to be his most trusted spiritual advisor, friend and confidant. It seemed so appropriate to dedicate this piece to her with eternal gratitude for her love and guidance! In nature, each butterfly goes through four stages in its life: 1) egg, 2) larva/caterpillar, 3) pupa, and 4) adult. During each stage, the butterfly's appearance changes and it leads a completely different kind of life. This development process is called metamorphosis. Just as the butterfly works through these four stages, so do human beings in both their physical and spiritual life. As a butterfly soars and dips in flight, so does a human being in his or her final transition of life.

## Topaz Nocturne

This nocturne is a gentle, yet expansive piece, which reflects the great love that Darren felt for friends and family during his short lifetime. He was born on Friday, November 1 (All Saints Day), and one of his birthstones is the topaz. "Topaz Nocturne" obviously should be played with a warm, singing touch. Be careful to shape the RH countermelody in measures 7–10, balancing it with the melody line in the top voice. The piece builds to an expansive climax in measure 28. One might wish to place an agogic accent (—) on the downbeat of measure 28 to give this chord special significance.

## Forever in Our Hearts

When I arrived at this last piece in the book, it seemed appropriate to compose some kind of epilogue that would, in essence, summarize my feelings of love for Darren and loss over his untimely departure. The music just seemed to flow out effortlessly, and before I knew it, the piece was finished. It was at this point in time that I came to the realization that every piece in the collection had a "rising" motive; then I was also somewhat startled to realize that the last notes ended on measure 23. Darren was 23 years old when he passed away. Perhaps he was there to guide me all along! Thank you, Darren, for providing all the love and inspiration that allowed this book to happen. You will indeed be "Forever in Our Hearts."